My Australian Animal Book

by Heidi Damman

MY AUSTRALIAN ANIMAL BOOK
Copyright © 2018 by Heidi Damman
All rights reserved. No part of this book may be used or reproduced in any manner whatsoever without written permission.
For information contact:
Heidi Damman at www.heididamman.com
ISBN: 978-0-6484183-0-6
First Edition 2018

for Chloe, Katelyn and Emma

Wombat

Kookaburra

Blue-tongue Lizard

Dingo

Lyrebird

Tasmanian Devil

Heidi Damman is a mother of three children and has been an early childhood educator for ten years. She is incorporating her love of the Australian environment and her creative abilities to inspire a love of Australian animals in children.

www.ingramcontent.com/pod-product-compliance
Lightning Source LLC
Chambersburg PA
CBHW061818290426
44110CB00026B/2911